MW00886621

THE SILENCED MUSES
A TESTIMONY TO LIFE. NOT DEATH.

By
Neringa Danienė

Translated from Lithuanian
By
Laima Vincė

ISBN: 9781729488133

SETTING: The play is set in Lithuanian in 1940 – 1941. Lithuania is first occupied by the Soviet Union, and then Nazi Germany.

MATILDA OLKIN
NOAH OLKIN – Matilda's father
ASNA OLKIN – Matilda's mother
ILYA – Matilda's brother
MIKA – Matilda's sister
GRUNIA – Matilda's sister

1 NARRATOR
LUCY– Childhood friend

2 NARRATOR
ALDONA – Classmate (Kupiškis)
ALDUTĖ – The little girl who witnesses the murders

3 NARRATOR
ELENA – Childhood friend
ADA – Classmate (Rokiškis)
LANDLADY
GENOVAITĖ – Grunia's friend, a little girl

4 NARRATOR
VAIČIONIS – Matilda's classmate
1 WHITE ARMBANDER

5 NARRATOR
2 WHITE ARMBANDER

NARRATORS - CHILDREN, NEIGHBORS, STUDENTS,
OTHERS

PROLOGUE

In the center of the stage there is a table. On the back stage wall there are three abstract panels. All manner of objects are displayed there. Stage front there are two easels, one stage left, and one stage right. At the front of the stage there are seven chairs in a row. Black and white photographs are arranged on the center chair.

GRUNIA emerges out of the audience and climbs onto the stage. She is carrying a bouquet of white lilies.

GRUNIA:
>Was it true, or was it a story?
>I don't know...
>I saw three sisters walking,
>Three sisters I saw.

>>Armfuls of flowers they carried,
>>Much sunshine and flowers.
>>Their hair was blond and braided,
>>And their eyes were blue.

>Then someone carried off
>The Sun and all the flowers.
>The young sisters left
>For foreign lands.

>>Then I saw their tears,
>>And their sorrow I saw...
>>Was it true, or was it a story?
>>I don't know.

1 NARRATOR *(stands up from her seat in the audience)*: Between the two World Wars in the town of Rokiškis (just like in every other Lithuanian town and village) half of the population was Jewish.

All the actors rise out of the audience and walk on stage. They take their seats in the chairs. The teenagers and children stand behind the chairs. GRUNIA decorates the easels with lillies.

4 NARRATOR: Since ancient times Lithuanian Jews, or Litvaks, were merchants. It could not have been any other way because under the Tsars they could not own land. Therefore, the greater part of the twon of Rokiškis's shops, factories, and workshops belonged to Jews.

2 NARRATOR *(reads from a newspaper)*: In 1933 the newspaper, *The Echo of Lithuania*, reported in an article titled, "The Jewish Community of Rokiškis" that "Lithuanians and Jews can be commended on how well they live together as one community."

5 NARRATOR *(reads from a newspaper)*: The monthly journal, "The Municipality" writes that out of twelve seats on the local government, five were occupied by Jews.

2 NARRATOR *(reads from a newspaper)*: That same year *The Echo of Lithuania* writes that "The Jews of Rokiškis participated in the fight for Lithuanian independence from Tsarist Russia. A Lithuanian Jew from Rokiškis, Rabbi Samuel Sniegas, was on the first committee formed to defend Lithuania's independence.

Later he became the chaplain for Jews in the Lithuanian army. A whole book could be written about the good work this man accomplished in his lifetime.

5 NARRATOR *(reads from a newspaper)*: The successful Jewish lawyer from Rokiškis, Noah Trifkinas, was awarded a medal of the third order of Vytautas the Great.

8 NARRATOR (ASNA): Between the two World Wars Jewish cultural life was active in Rokiškis. There was a Yiddish theater and Jewish schools. At the same time many Jewish children studied in Lithuanian schools.

The actors stand and point to photographs of the Jewish community that are hanging on the back wall.

3 NARRATOR: On Synagogue Street there were three wooden synagogues. There was one more synagogue on the street that is now called Sauna Street. The three synagogues were painted each in one of the colors of the Lithuanian flag: yellow, green, and red.

6 NARRATOR (MATILDA): If you were to cross the street that was called Kamayu then, but which is now called Republic Street, you would find a building that was once the Jewish People's Bank. Now it is a funeral home.

7 NARRATOR (NOAH): One of the oldest, and largest, brick buildings in town back then was the Europa Hotel. Next door to the hotel there was a market. Many cultural events took place there. The Europa Hotel is still a hotel today.

8 NARRATOR (ASNA): The elders of Rokiškis still remember that in Independence Square once stood Sheras's Pharmacy. Sheras not only sold medicine, but generously shared advice with his customers. He could help you through any illness. Now in the old pharmacy building there is a bank and a shopping mall.

4 NARRATOR: On the other side of Independence Square were a number of shops owned by Lord Tyzenhaus. Many Jews rented shop space there. He built the complex of shops to expand business, so that the town would grow and expand. Thanks to this strategy, Rokiškis developed not as an agricultural town, but as an industrial town.

1 NARRATOR: Even today in Independence Square you may notice the home of the Zametas family, the owners of the metal works, "Litmetal." People in Rokiškis refer to it as "The House with the Towers." The Zametas family lived on the second floor. He rented the first floor to shopkeepers. It must be noted that Zametas was even the town mayor.

10 NARRATOR (MIKA): On the corner of Independence Square, where the social security office is now located, lived the Gandelman family. They were a family of respected doctors.

9 NARRATOR (ILYA): On the other side of the street the famous lawyer, Trifkinas, who we already mentioned before, built a beautiful brick house. He was the same man who received the medal of honor. There is a library in that house today.

5 NARRATOR: On Vytautas Street there stood a hotel called The London. It was owned and operated by Meleras. The Meleras brothers also owned a printing press, and cardboard, saccharine, and candy factories. The people who worked there back then remember that they had very warm ties with the factory owners.

Part 1
CHILDHOOD

We hear the sound of a train whistle. The actors stand and begin taking down the photographs from the back panels and arranging them onto the easels. The sound of the train whistle fades. Gradually the narrators become their characters. The narrators picks up the chairs one by one and set them in their places.

2 NARRATOR: A few Jewish families lived beside the train station in the small agricultural town of Panemunėlis, not far from the larger town of Rokiškis. They were small merchants who lived harmoniously with their local Lithuanians neighbors. They shared daily routines with one another and celebrated all their holidays together.

1 NARRATOR: The older generation of Panemunėlis to this day most vividly remembers the family of the local pharmacist, Noah Olkin. There are still many legends told about the Olkins even now.

4 NARRATOR: Noah Olkin was a sensitive man. He was honest. And he was wise. He would help anyone who reached out to him. He would counsel people who were ill and help them in any way he could. He even gave away medicine to the poor. *(Noah Olkin sits down in a chair center stage)*.

3 NARRATOR: Asna Okin was a housewife. She raised her children and tended to their home. (Asna Olkin sits down in a chair besides Noah). The Olkins had four children. The oldest son was Ilya (a very handsome young man) and the three daughters were called Matilda, Mika, and Grunia. *(The four children stand behind their parents).*

5 NARRATOR: The Okin family ate breakfast, lunch, and dinner together. From the time when they were little, the Olkins taught their children to be honest, to work hard, to help others, and to feel empathy. The Olkins wished for their children to grow up and study in the university and to become good citizens of Lithuania.

2 NARRATOR: Not a single one of the Okin's neighbors ever heard the family arguing in public.

5 NARRATOR: Olkin enjoyed reading all the great Russian writers. He read Lermontov, Pushkin, Nekrasov, and Dostoyevsky.

4 NARRATOR: Although he was a Jew, Olkin respected his Catholic neighbors and supported the Church. He was a close friend of Father Matelionis, the priest at the Panemunėlis Church. Every Sunday after mass Father Matelionis came to tea at the Olkin's house. Noah Olkin donated an oak confessional to the Church.

ELENA (*stands and takes off her shoes*): I went to their synagogue a few times. But I was little then and I didn't like it much. It wasn't fancy like our church. I would tell my Jewish girlfriends that I thought our church was much prettier than their house of worship.

2 NARRATOR: Elena Petronytė, the Olkin girls' playmate.

All the children kick off their shoes and begin to play with the stones on stage. NOAH OLKIN takes the newspaper from NARRATOR 2 and sits down at the table. He begins to read the newspaper. ASNA OLKIN works on embroidering a tablecloth.

2 NARRATOR: The Olkin children ran around the town's streets together with all the other neighborhood children. They would go swimming in the Šetekšna River, play games that they made up themselves, and together attended the local elementary school.

4 NARRATOR: The Olkin's house stood right beside thc street. On the opposite side of the street stood a mill that belonged to their good friend, Marcel Neniškis.

LUCY (*stands and kicks off her shoes*): My grandmother's best friend was Asna Olkin.

2 NARRATOR: Lucy Neniškis was the granddaughter of the miller, Marcel Neniškis, and his wife, Anel. She would come from Kaunas to spend the summer holidays with her grandparents. Lucy was the Olkin girls' best friend.

The children call out Lucy's name.

LUCY **(joins the game***):* I knew all the members of the Olin family very well. I spent all the summers of my youth and childhood in Panemunėlis. Not a single summer went by when all three Olkin girls wouldn't stand on train platform waiting for my train to arrive from Kaunas. I was closest to Mika. We all called her the amazing Mindochka. **(She hugs Mika)** Hands down, she was our leader. She came up with all sorts of games for us to play. We never played with dolls. We made up our own games.

Music plays.

5 NARRATOR: Noah Olkin let the children keep a bulletin board on the outside wall of the pharmacy. The children, though mostly Mika, would post notices announcing the grand opening of new streets on that bulletin board.

Mika hangs up a notice on the bulletin board. They all read it. They run to the edge of the stage.

LUCY: We would read the bulletin and then run to the place where the opening was about to take place. Mika would be the master of ceremonies.

Mika tugs a white ribbon out of Grunia's hair. She pulls a pair of scizzors out of her dress pocket. She hands the scizzors to the girls.

MIKA: I honorably name this street, "Dirt Street."

LUCY: When Mika gave the signal, we would cut the ribbon.

The children cut the ribbon and clap.

ELENA: When I was little, I would play pharmacy with the Olkin girls.

The children run to the opposite side of the stage. They arrange the stones on the easels.

ELENA: Mr. Olkin would give us empty medicine bottles and boxes. We would take them and play pharmacy all day long.
ILYA: Hey, I need some medicine for diarrhea.

The girls laugh and chase after ILYA. The men turn the table over and the children climb inside and play.

4 NARRATOR: The children would run inside Lucy's grandfather's mill and play court among the long boards. Whoever, according to their child logic, was guilty of crime would stand trial.

LUCY: Most of the time Ilya would be found guilty. Usually for stealing candy. And for other things too... Matilda would play the judge and Mika would play the lawyer. One time Mika sentenced a child to the death penalty.

GRUNIA hearing these words is frightened and startles. She is holding a pile of stones in her apron. She lets the apron go and stones fall out onto the stage floor. The girls rush to comfort her. They lead her to the table. They begin a new game, newspaper.

2 NARRATOR:	The children decided to publish their own newspaper. They called it *The Panemunėlis News*. On Saturdays, during the Sabbath, they invited their guests to read their newspaper for the price of a few coins. With those coins they would buy caramels.
LUCY:	Before we published our newspaper, we would run around the town getting all the latest news. Every time a passenger tran neared the station we would run to meet it. We would find out who was coming back on the train and who was leaving. We knew who was receiving visitors and who was leaving. The newspaper needed comics and poems. Matilda wrote the poems and Mika wrote the news. She wrote a hilarious article about a May picnic on the river. I remember one funny article that Mika called, "The Lost Pig." The main character was a pig who got away from its owner and ran all over town.

The children laugh. Mika hangs the newspaper on the bulletin board. They all gather around to read.

2 NARRATOR:	Lucy, Mika, Grunia, and Matilda waited eagerly every summer for Lucy's Aunt Teofilia to arrive. She would bring ten meters of colorful fabric from the city of Kaunas with her. With that fabric Lucy's grandmother Anel would sew all four girls identical dresses.

ASNA OLKIN spreads out a tablecloth. The children wash their feet and enter the room.

2 NARRATOR: Not only were the children best of friends, but so were the Olkin and the Neniškis families. They shared everything they had. Anel would bring the Olkins cheese and butter. The children ate their lunch at the Olkin's house and their dinner at the Neniškis's.

LUCY: When we were at the Olkin house we were careful to keep it very clean. You would never find dust under their beds.

ELENA: On Passover our Jewish neighbors always made ginger cookies for us and gave us matzahs. Over all, the Jewish ladies baking was very tasty. Even the simplest recipes, like carrot cake, tasted best when they made them. Their baked goods just melted in your mouth. Lithuanian women, even the richest ones, the best housewives, did not know how to bake like that.

The men enter the room.

2 NARRATOR (*stands*): On Saturdays, during the Sabbath, nobody worked. The Olkins invited all their neighbors to their home on the Sabbath—Doctor Sadaukas, the teacher, Jonas Siminonis, Father Matelionis, the teacher, Stasė Valavičiūtė, and others. Mr. Olkin would rely on the children's creativity to provide the entertainment.

Quiet music plays. The children stand in a row stage front. The adults sit at the table and listen.

MATILDA: Oh, the Sun has woken
And leaps from her bed.
She opens one eye, then the other,
"Good morning!"

GRUNIA: And all the flowers rejoice,
All the flowers and the birds.
They call out one after the other,
"Good morning!"

MIKA: And out into the wide dewey meadow
The girl sends the herd.
And the flowers greet her,
And the Sun, and the birds.

MATILDA: And everywhere it's just the Sun...
The Sun—riding in her chariot across the sky,
The Sun—diving into the brook,
The Sun—in every blossom,
The Sun—in every cup;
Every drop of dew...

LUCY: But the Sun shines most
In the eyes of the little girl.
Her eyes are bright, full of light.
They greet her joyful world,
A world bursting to life, filled with sunshine.
"Good morning! Good morning!"

The guests clap. NOAH OLKIN carries in a record player. He puts on a record. Music plays a waltz. The parents dance, then the children join in, and then the others.

The narrators returns to their places on the chairs. Only LUCY remains. The children carry in three large white pillows and lie down. MATILDA sings a lullaby in Yiddish. She holds sheets of papers with poems in her hands.

4 NARRATOR: Matilda, the Olkin's second born, was somehow different from the others.

3 NARRATOR: Matilda like to be alone. She reacted with great senstivity to even the smallest thing. When the children played, she would stand and watch.

LUCY: Matilda was a few years older than me. Often, her father would make her stay at home and write poems. Only after she had written a poem would her father let her out to play. Why he did that, I don't know?

MATILDA *(stands and quietly climbs down from the stage. She hops around as she works out the rhythm of a poem):*

My window is so small,
So small and cozy.
Sun, the land, waves of gold,
Sun, the land, and the sky.

If you wish—you may see
The land, the sky—
A sparrow twirling on a dahlia,
And on the dahlia—three blooms.

Part 2
SCHOOL

Matilda's poems lie on the table in a noisy classroom. The children put on their shoes. They gather around a table. Matilda and Aldona are seated at the table. Other children stand near the bulletin board and make noise.

1 NARRATOR: Matilda completed her studies at the Panemunėlis Elementary School with honors. She went on the study at the Kupiškis Gymnasium.

ALDONA: Matilda was a pretty girl with dark hair and dark eyes, but with milky white skin. She had a cheerful personality. Although she was Jewish, she spoke Lithuanian without any accent. In Kupiškis we all knew that Matilda was a poet and that impressed us deeply. We were very interested in her and in her poetry.

5 NARRATOR: Aldona, Matilda's classmate, Kupiškis.

ALDONA: A few of her poems were published in the magazine *Little Star*. We all read her poems. Matilda's poetry, her thoughts, her work, was all very Lithuanian. She was just like the rest of us Lithuanian children. She would write about our holidays. It made no difference to us that she was Jewish.

1 NARRATOR: It was the same when she transferred to the high school in Rokiškis.

The students cross over to the opposite side of the stage. ADA sits down beside MATILDA in ALDONA'S place.

5 NARRATOR: Some Jewish children studied successfully at the Lithuanian language high schools. Here the school observed the Sabbath and they were not required to take exams or do homework on Saturdays.

1 NARRATOR: Matilda's classmate, Ada Apuokaitė, Rokiškis.

ADA: Matilda was cheerful and friendly. Her gaze always seemed to be somewhere distant, and not engaged in the petty details of school life. She seemed to be flying above everything. Often during breaks she would stand and gaze out the classroom window for a long time with her hands tucked under her apron. What she was thinking, I don't know

ADA snatches the poem MATILDA is composing away from her, teasing her. She runs to the edge of the stage and reads it out loud. The other students gather around.

ADA: Now I live, let's say, like the Czechs.
(If I'm not mistaken, that's what he wrote)
But I write:
Now I live, let's say in Rokiškis,
In the cross street near Bernadette's.
Through one window I see five apple trees.
Through the other I see Bernadette's house and the church steeple—
And a garden besides. And something else
One usually does not mention in poems.

It's an interesting neighborhood where we live.
Narrow Street is right here, and Sauna Street, and North Street.
All the eighth graders take shelter here—
And me as well. I sit and study Goethe's biography.

MATILDA *(climbing up onto a chair)*:
So you see it goes like this:
They told me to tell this story—
but I didn't know how.
After, there were consequences.
And the beginning of the new school year was scandalous.
And I live, let's say, in Rokiškis,
And I analyze Goethe, as such...
Narrow Street 3 is my address
In the neighborhood where all we eighth graders
live.

Matilda jumps off the chair and walks down stage. The children snatch the poem and pin it to the bulletin board.

ADA: I never saw her sitting alone during the breaks studying. Her attitudes towards grades was very balanced.

1 NARRATOR: Matilda's inner life opened up in all its beauty. Poems simply burst out of her. While she was a high school student in Rokiškis she published her poems in magazines for young people, like *Little Star*, or the Catholic magazines *The Future* and *Sunrays of the Future*.

ADA *(reads the poem):* I remember the editor of *Little Star* wrote a letter to Matilda Olkin: "We are waiting and waiting for the fruits of your cheerful pen."

The children pin the newspaper to the bulletin board.

1 NARRATOR: Not a single literary evening at our high school passed with out Matilda and her poems taking the lead.

ADA: Matilda's poems were light, easy to understand, and full of her joy for life.

5 NARRATOR: One of her poems, which she dedicated to Lithuania, became a song.

The children stand in a row stage front and sing the poem.

ALL:
Many roads lead to the sun—
Thousands of boulevards!
You walk. Striding forwards
Along those wide road.

You carry a pure loving heart
For Lithuania.
I hear your words ring out
Like a bright prayer.

Wide fields filled with song,
Hymns to Lithuania.
And your word, Your word
Is eternal.

A heart, loving and pure,
You carry for Lithuania.
I hear your words ring out
Like a bright prayer.

1 NARRATOR: In September 1939 Matilda Olkin was accepted into the Faculty of Philology at the University of Vytautas the Great in Kaunas. After a few months, the univeristy was transferred to Vilnius. Matilda went to live in Vilnius.

5 NARRATOR: At the same time Europe went to war.

Part 3
YOUTH

We hear the sound of a train whistle. The table is turned around. On the table there is a tablecloth and a record player. The NARRATORS return to their places on the chairs. NOAH and ASNA OLKIN sit at the table. Their children sit on the floor around them. The are all reading newspapers. The children are barefoot.

4 NARRATOR: After she finished the first year of her studies, Matilda returned home to Panemunėlis for the summer. Times were difficult and chaotic, both in the world and in the Olkin's household, and in Matilda's heart.

LUCY: Matilda kept a diary. There she wrote her poems, and there she wrote down her thoughts.

MATILDA hangs a calendar on the bulletin board. She tears off a page from the calendar.

MATILDA: It's been a strange summer this year. It seems as though everything were passing and will soon be gone forever. Whenever I part with my love, I feel as though I will never see him again...
In the evenings Papa always says: "One more day has passed."

NOAH: One more day has passed...

MATILDA: One more day has passed and I haven't accomplished anything. I must admit, I enjoy arguing with Papa. Our arguments are cultured and rarely escalate beyond the norms of civility. Papa is worried about my future. But I just grab hold of a few cliches to make my point. Papa is deeply hurt that I am not writing now. I just find some justification, which I don't believe myself and nobody else does either.

I sometimes think, what does our home lack? How I suffer on those days when everyone walks around as though electrified and each one of us lets off sparks. But it passes easily. *(she places a record on the record player and we hear a waltz playing)* All we need to do is to lay a pretty white tablecloth down on the dinner table, set the table nicely, light the lamp—and then Papa, when he hears a Strauss waltz playing, begins conducting the music with his hands, and then invites one of us daughters to dance with him.

NOAH OLKIN begins to dance a waltz with MIKA, then with MATILDA. ILYA dances with GRUNIA.

MATILDA *(dancing with NOAH OLKIN):* The situation with money at home is very bad. But I try not to think about it. All morning long it rained. I went out in a summer dress and without any socks. Lucy borrowed my shoes and boots.

NOAH OLKIN dances with ASNA OLKIN.

MATILDA: Today I had a fight with Mika. Mika shouted at me.

MIKA: "I hate you because you are too good!"

MATILDA: No, I'm not good. I'm just bland—bland in love and bland in hate. Today I received a letter *(pulls out the letter)* and I just about cried. Not one smile, not one gentle word. It is so obvious, so obvious. He does not love me.

Matilda pins the letter to the bulletin board. The music grows quiet.

2 NARRATOR: Matilda experienced her first love.

LUCY: Sheras, the son of the Rokiškis pharmacist, fell in love with Matilda. He was tall and had curly hair. He was very interested in Matilda.

MATILDA *(To Lucy):* I wanted to read him a poem in French today, but already by the second line I sensed that he was not interested. So I stopped reading. After such moments, when he asks me if I would agree to leave everything behind and run away with him, his words seem painful to me, and I feel as though he were making fun of me. *(walks over to GRUNIA, who is playing with stones).*

LUCY: Matilda did not care much for Sheras.

MATILDA (*To Grunia*):It's no good. Will I always love like this? If my love were here, I'd snuggle up to him and I would cry. But he would not understand me because he does not love me. I don't tell anyone that. It is better for them not to know.

NOAH exits. MATILDA tears off another page from the calendar.

MATILDA *(dancing):* If I had to say what my mood is today, I would not know what to say. I've been dancing and singing so much that Mama begged me to be quiet.

ASNA: Be quiet, Matilda, please, I beg of you.

MATILDA*(dancing):* I've decided to follow a new tactic. Honestly. Wasn't my previous role ridiculous? To sit and daydream and to love and to suffer. And it all means nothing to him. And if I kiss him, it will be the same sort of friendly kiss I give to Lucy or any of my other friends. Enough. I am setting down a limit and I say: this love is over. After all, I have ambitions of my own. I will be strong. I will not let him play around with me.

NOAH walks on stage with more newspapers. Everyone takes a newspaper and beging to read.

MATILDA *(still dancing):* Papa returned from Panevėžys worried and nervous. Our home is threatened with being dissolved. It's starvation, plain and simple.

ILYA slams his fist on the table in anger. He storms out and slides down and sits with his back against the wall.

MATILDA: No! I will work. Everything will be alright. *(She stops dancing. She walks to the very edge of the stage down front. At first she whispers, but then her voice grows steadily louder)* Times are awful. The world has spilled out into the streets. People shove a red handkerchief into their pocket and shout. Salomėja Nėris, Liudas Giras—I cannot fathom how normal people can write that way. There are banners and more banners everywhere. The biggest communist, if there were such a one who is a cultured person, would not be able to stand it. I often think about how people lack culture. Could it even be possible for communism and its ideology to be expressed in poems that are not dominated by destruction, but by creativity, not by hate, but by love?

It is so difficult for me. I'd like to utter one word.
That unspoken word trembles within me.
I see processions, generations, gliding past.
And a blue longing and shivering suffering.

> And joy, quivering in tiny rays of light,
> And the pain of aeons of shattered hopes.
> But I—am that unspoken word and shadow.
> I carry that unspoken word in my heart.

It is so difficult for me. I would just like to utter that one word.
Just one word for the crowds and for the nations.
The processions would pause. Time would come to a halt.
All the generations would stop, and listen.

> And my word would flutter above the mountains and the seas.
> Above flowing rivers and rough waters.
> And longing and trembling suffering would cease,
> And the pain of aeons of shattered hopes.

Everyone stares at MATILDA shocked and silent.

MATILDA *(as though trying to justify her odd behavior)*:
> I received a letter from him. It was gentle and good. I thought that His letter would be cold and official, like His last one. I had already prepared my mood for that, my cold mood. But now, when I read His letter, which was so warm, but at the same time so full of restlessness, I felt guilty.

MATILDA pulls off another page from the calendar. She turns around and sees NOAH carrying out the record player. ASNA is on the verge of tears. MATILDA sits down besides LUCY and MIKA.

MATILDA:
> Yesterday I had a talk with mama. At first we were kidding around, but then the talk got serious.

ASNA:
> When are you getting married?

MATILDA:
> Nobody is thinking about marriage.

ASNA:
> If you are not thinking about marriage, then you should not be sitting on his bed.

The girls giggle. NOAH enters carrying a newspaper. The all gather around him.

MATILDA:
> Today it is exactly one year since the war began. The newspapers have marked the occasion by writing their headlines all in capital letters. It's horrific, when you think about it.

What I should do is sit down and work on editing several poems. Oh, that poetry collection of mine! I am working on it with no inspiration, knowing that no one will publish it anyway. There is nothing in my poems that is relevant. I write about the pain of suffering over centuries at time when we are required to sing about how happy we are right now and about our bright tomorrow.

MATILDA tears off one more page from the calendar. LUCY hugs MIKA. She says goodbye and she leaves.

MATILDA: Everyone at home is in a bad mood. It's about the Neniškises. They are leaving everything they own behind and they are leaving. Lucy promised to come back and visit us.

LUCY *(leaving)*:   I promise.

MATILDA: Lucy has left. We all cried. It was so painful to say good-bye to her. With Lucy gone all my summer joy, all my sun, is gone. Where are you now, my love? One time while I was writing Him a letter this question burst forth and I wrote it in my letter. I received this reply.

4 NARRATOR: You ask me where I am? I am in my room and I am eating chocolate.

MATILDA: He did not understand my question.

The girls clutch pillows and lie down, putting their heads down on the pillows. MATILDA looks for comfort from GRUNIA.

MATILDA: I am a fool. Millions of people in the world are dying. People are starving. The war is moving closer towards us. I may not receive my stipend —nothing is certain, everything is in a fog. And I am standing on the edge of a precipice picking at the petals of a daisy, asking: Love me? Loves me not? It is foolish and naive.

MATILDA sings GRUNIA a lullaby. GRUNIA falls asleep. MATILDA stands quietly and walks to her pillow. She prepares to sleep, but then remembers something.

MATILDA: I know those mornings all too well when Papa, after drinking his cup of tea with milk, goes out somewhere and comes back agitated, biting his nails. And Mama stares at him with fear in her eyes and does not say anything.

Who to borrow money from? From Rachel? From Petronis? From Elijudis? From Vaitkūnas? From Mrs. Meyers...

At tea I was frightened for mama. She gazed at me with that frozen glance and her eyes filled with tears. It's like that all the time. Then Papa began talking about how we will need to sell the house, again.

NOAH: We must sell the house.

MATILDA: I see how Mama trembles, ever so slightly. It seems as though it's not a house that will be divided in two, but my heart, torn into two pieces.

I read the newspapers. The people who write those newspapers don't believe in anything they write themselves. They write about the new literature, supposedly a literature where everyone can grow and evolve... Grow and evolve. But at the same time the limits that are set for this new literature are so narrow, so simple, and I'd say, not creative at all. It's the path of social realism... If there's a comic depicting priests, then they must of necessity have giant stomachs and an obsession with cards. If they show a spiritual person, then that person must appear foolish and corrupt. If they show a worker, then that worker must be ill and unhappy. Literature is now free to grow and evolve! It is sad and ludicrous.

We hear the sound of a train approaching. Everyone awakens. MATILDA puts on her shoes. She packs the tablecloth into her pillow along with papers, the calendar, Grunia's stone. MIKA takes off her red ribbon and puts it in the pillowcase. MATILDA walks down stage. She stands there. The table is turned around. The family sits down around ILYA.

Part 4
VILNIUS

The train whistle grows softer. The LANDLADY meets MATILDA. She looks MATILDA over from head to toe. MATILDA shyly unwraps her things from the tablecloth. She looks around. The LANDLADY glares at her and then exists.

MATILDA: Twenty days have passed since I last unlocked my diary. I'm in Vilnius. I have a new room. The walls are painted blue. Ilya is off with some sort of Communist Party matters. He's forgotten all about his studies. Liza is smiling all the time with her pink-painted lips. And then there is Him, my one and only, who I kissed and loved yesterday, and who loves me back, and who is my only comfort in my gray life, so empty of creativity... But Him, who I am growing closer and closer to as each day passes. He says he loves me and I believe Him. I want to believe Him and I must believe Him.

Yesterday we spent the entire day together. Yesterday was a sacred day, a great day.

But today I don't know.

MATILDA begins to unpack and set out her things. The LANDLADY enters and circles around the room, watching MATILDA.

MATILDA: I spend every day at the university. It's always the same people—they are neither good nor bad. That same worry worm is eating away at me. I often feel so small and so worthless. I am not pretty. Especially not these days. My face is white and my nose is red. My student cap looks awful on me. *(She picks up Grunia's stone and gazes at it)* What is happening at home? Worries, worries, and more worries...

MATILDA hangs up her calendar. She tears off a page. ILYA enters the room. He takes MIKA'S red ribbon from the pile of MATILDA'S things and ties it onto her arm.

MATILDA: They have nationalized our pharmacy.The matter of money is especially painful for me. What will happen if I don't receive my stipend? Ilya told me to go get a job...

The LANDLADY walks through the room in a threatening manner.

ILYA: Matilda, it's serious, go get a job.

MATILDA: Ilya tells me to get a job. Papa encourages me to get a job.

NOAH: Matilda!

MATILDA: Sheras suggests I get a job (*4 NARRATOR nods his head*) Mama begs me to get a job.

ASNA: Matilda.

MATILDA: How do I run away from my own black shadow? Should I cry? No. Should I laugh and have fun here at university with Liza. No one should know that my days have never been as hard as they are now, and that I am so close to this bottomless abyss. *(MATILDA begins to dance).*

My last 50 lits, which will run out soon.

He promised to write to me today.

Ilya is preparing for the October Revolution parade. He has a lot of work to do.

My room is so cold.

The phone is ringing. Is it for me? It's for Ilya.

ILYA exits. MATILDA is freezing cold. She grabs the tablecloth and wraps it around her shoulders. Dancing a hysterical dance, she recites a poem.

Oh, how many have gathered
In my home of mourning.
I hold an infant in my arms,
And my infant—is Death.

They brought a silver sash
And armfuls of lilies, white.
And I cannot thank them,
And I cannot smile.

All around me are lilies, white, white,
And faces wearing bright smiles.
But my hands are so cold.
A black ribbon is tied in my hair.

Someone has trampled my love—
The whitest of the white blossoms.
And among the wilted lilies,
I see them, I speak to them.

Oh, how many have gathered
And not one will see love.
I hold an infant in my arms--
And my infant—is Death.

MATILDA stops dancing and stands in front of the calendar. She tries to collect herself. She hastily tears off a few pages. Each time she tears off a page, she pauses, grows more and more serious.

MATILDA *(coldly and calmly:* That pain that I thought would kill me has passed. I work hard, although it is hard to work. I study. I write cheerful letters home. I am carefree and cheerful towards everyone. Tomorrow I am going to a dance. And all that just so that I would forget.

She tears a page from the calendar. She wraps the tablecloth around her shoulders like a shawl. She puts on a false smile. With a sheaf of papers in her hands she walks to the edge of the stage. After a pause, she takes a deep breath. She is serious.

MATILDA: I just spent two happy hours at a literary evening. I read my poems and the audience's response was very warm. After I was finished reading, I ran out of the auditorium, not waiting for anyone. I did not feel like approaching anyone to talk, nor did I want anyone to approach me. I completely closed myself off inside. I don't trust anyone anymore.

If He could lie to me, what then...

Yesterday I saw Him walk past with Chaya. He kissed her in the hallway. But really, isn't it the same to me who He kisses? I no longer belong to Him.

You! *(to the audience)* You, who pried open my diary with your dirty fingernails, don't laugh at me! You can laugh about anything, you can turn anything into a joke, but don't laugh at my heart, and don't play with it either. *(Pause)* He played.

MATILDA places the papers on the table.

MATILDA: The landlady made my bad mood even worse. Her daughter came running in here.

2 NARRATOR: Mama is calling you!

The LANDLADY enters. She walks around MATILDA'S room, touching everything.

LANDLADY: How much do you want for a lesson? Are you sure you don't want more than that?

MATILDA: She was so sarcastic when I told her my fee for tutoring. I said to her, "I can find you a cheaper teacher."

LANDLADY: Thank you very much. We will find one ourselves.

LANDLADY exits.

MATILDA: The landlady has a blue and red nose and applies her lipstick crooked. She beats her husband. Interesting woman!

She takes down her calendar and sits at the table. She tears off a page.

MATTILDA: Wednesday I returned home from the university and there was no letter for me. I had to lean on the wall, so that I would not collapse in tears. *(She tears off a page from the calendar)* He came *(tears off a page)*.

"Do you want to break up with me?" I asked Him. "No," he said. Only both of us know that we must. He says he loves me. Should I believe him?

MATILDA places the pillow on the table. She puts her head on the pillow and wraps the tablecloth around her.

MATILDA: Yesterday I spent the day writing down the names of families of the Red Army for the elections. All day long I suffered their stench and filthy smells. The women are ugly and have vulgar enormous chests. When I returned to my room, where it was clean and bright, I was overwhelmed with the feeling that I would like to have a loving husband and a dear baby of my own *(sits down and takes the tablecloth and wraps it into the shape of a swaddled infant. She holds the infant to her chest and rocks the imaginary baby).*

Yes—if I had a bay of my own, I would calm down. I would like a to have a healthy, beautiful baby, one with brown eyes, or with blue eyes, like His...

My tiny little baby
Why can't you fall asleep?
Longing overwhelms you tonight.
Longing crouches beside your cradle.

> The nights are long and dark,
> And the road leads far into the distance.
> On such a night you will leave me,
> My tiny little baby.

And suffering will wait for you beside the gate,
Like a beloved friend.
Great suffering and hardship
Will carry you silently through long generations.

> Long generations carry suffering
> From the cradle to the grave—
> Suffering immense and deep,
> And as endless as the night.

Fall asleep now. It is a long road
That will lead you into the night...
Go to sleep. I will sing to you,
My tiny little baby.

MATILDA lies down and sings a lullby. She drifts off to sleep. Enter LUCY.

LUCY :   Sheras bought Matilda a pair of fancy shoes.

MATILDA jumps up, awake. She grabs a pair of shoes and shows them to LUCY. The LANDLADY walks past them scornfully.

MATILDA:	Yesterday when I came back from the university I found him here. He came to see me in the evening. He was hot. At one moment, I was afraid of him.

The both giggle. MATILDA takes a step forward. She admires the shoes. She feels good about herself.

LUCY:	But she was already in love with another student.
MATILDA*:*	I went to the opera. I sat beside Donka Segalis. He was trying to be interesting. To get my attention. I wore a red dress and my new shoes. Ita curled my hair before I left. I don't think I looked so bad.

MATILDA steps forwards to the edge of the stage. She gazes at her shoes. Then she suddenly yanks them off.

MATILDA:	Who am I kidding?

ILYA enters.

MATILDA:	Ilya came over. He told me about home. He told me everything was fine at home. He did it on purpose. He said it was all warm and good at home.
ILYA:	Home—warm and happy.
MATILDA:	Papa – has a government job.
ILYA:	Papa – working. Mama is healthy.

MATILDA: Oh, there have been so many times when my greatest dream was to see them happy! I lay on the sofa and ate the pastries Ilya brought from home and listened to him talk. I'm shocked at myself. I blame myself for growing away from home. I've grown away from everything that ties me to my childhood. Maybe it's because of all this worrying over money. I often go hungry. On freezing cold days I go out in my autumn jacket and freeze. Then my teeth hurt, and my head. I have almost nothing to wear.

Oh, all this will pass. It must pass.

LUCY: She wanted to return those shoes to Sheras. But, she didn't get the chance. The war started.

Part 5
WAR

We hear a train whistle. ILYA and LUCY exit. MATILDA hurries to pack her things.

5 NARRATOR: The Soviet occupation with all its brutality descended upon the Jews of Rokiškis. In June, 1941, the Soviets arrested merchants, tradesmen, and doctors and crammed then into cattle cars and sent them to death camps in the far reaches of Siberia. The Soviets had nationalized the Okin's pharmacy. The Olkins continued to live quietly. Fortunately, when the Soviet wave of arrests in June passed through Panemunėlis the Olkin family was spared.

2 NARRATOR: But then, in that same month, a few weeks later, the Nazis occupied Lithuania, pushing out the Soviets.

3 NARRATOR: When the war began in Lithuania, Matilda returned home to her native Panemunėlis.

MATILDA steps out to the front of the stage. The table is turned around. Two WHITE ARMBANDERS snatch up two little girls' white ribbons from the floor and tie them onto their arms. They tear all the papers off the bulletin board and nail up their own notice. The sound of the train whistle subsides.

1 NARRATOR: The Nazis played out the same plan in every Lithuanian town they took over. Panemunėlis was no exception.

2 WHITE ARMBANDER:All the Jewish families in Panemunėlis were arrested and held in the train station. Later, some were transferred to the Panemunėlis Manor stable.

1 NARRATOR: Among those who were arrested was the Pharmacist Noah Olkin and his family.

WHITE ARMBANDER 2 walks up to MATILDA. He looks her over menancingly. He grabs her bundle out of her arms and thrusts it onto the table. He tosses the tablecloth aside. He points to the floor. MATILDA takes the tablecloth and begins scrubbing the floor. The WHITE ARMBANDER sits down and sifts through MATILDA's belongings. GRUNIA enters. She begins playing with the stones.

1 NARRATOR: While she was held in the ghetto, Matilda's friend and classmate, Juozas Vaičionis, who was studying to become a priest, came to visit her. He had a plan. He wanted to hide Matilda with his relatives in Panevėžys.

VAIČIONIS *(stands):* I wanted to save Matilda Olkin. She had to live. She was such a gifted poet. When the white armbanders went out, I snuck in and I said to her, "Run away with me! I know people who will hide you."

Quietly, VAIČIONIS and MATILDA gaze at one another.

VAIČIONIS: But Matilda would not even answer me. She just kept on scrubbing the floors. I could not get her to talk. I could not get her to answer me when I insisted, "Why don't you want to run away from here?

1 NARRATOR: After the White Armbanders arrested the Olkins, Father Matelionis managed to rescue and hide Noah Olkin in the wooden rectory beside the church for a few days. Late one night, when everyone was sleeping, Mr. Olkin went out for a walk and saw a notice written by the Nazis, stating that anyone caught hiding Jews would be executed.

GENOVAITĖ (*standing*): Mr. Olkin was terrified that someone might betray his friend, Father Matelionis, and that his friend would be shot. He went and turned himself in to the Nazis that very night.

The WHITE ARMBANDERS circle around GENOVAITĖ, looking her over. They circle around the other NARRATORS, who sit with their heads bent. They stop in front of NARRATOR 4. He stands and offers the WHITE ARMBANDERS a cigarette. Then, he ties a white ribbon around his arm. They both pick up the newspapers from the table and fold them into hats. They smoke.

1 NARRATOR: Genovaitė was twelve years old when the Nazis occupied the town. Every day her mother sent her to the stable with a horse-drawn wagon filled with soup and food for the Jewish families. Genovaitė tried to convince Matilda to run away with her and hide, but Matilda refused.

GENOVAITĖ: One time I came and I saw Matilda standing in the doorway. She looked sad and was deep in thought. Her younger sister, my friend, Grunia, stood beside her. Grunia said to me: "Are they going to shoot us?"

GRUNIA: They won't shoot us? Will they?

GENOVAITĖ: Without even hesitating I said to her, "Grunia, who would ever shoot a child?"

ALDUTĖ *(stands):* But the next day.

Part 6
DEATH

The music grows louder and louder.

1 NARRATOR:	On the road that leads out of Panemunėlis towards Kavoliškis a farmer named Petras Šarkauskas lived with his family. The farm and the farm house stood up on a hill close to a bend in the road. From their farm, they could see everything.
	The hired farm hand, Bronius, noticed a group of White Armbanders riding past on bicycles early in the morning.
ALDUTĖ:	They began to dig ditches in the forest early that morning. They did not have much success because tree roots prevented them from digging very deep. So, they gave it up and took their shovels to the other side of the road and began digging in the boggy land that belonged to the Kavoliškis manor. There was good land there and the grass grew well. Father had already mowed down the hay.
	Then they left only to return shortly afterwards, riding bicycles alongside a wagonload of people pulled by two horses over the rutted road. An armed guard sat at the front of the wagon and at the back. More armed men rode alongside the wagon on bicycles. The captives' heads were bowed. They had been blindfolded.
1 NARRATOR:	Aldutė was eight years old at the time.

The music grows louder. The White Armbanders rise. Threatingly they walk closer and closer to the girls, who step backwards away from them. The White Armbanders roughly grab their pillows out of their arms. Finally, the girls move behind the panels, hidden from view. All the others move back together with them behind the panels. As she talks, ALDUTĖ, crawls hides under the table and watches intently.

ALDUTĖ: After a few hours the men on bicycles disappeared. Then, an hour later, Bronius came and told us that a horse-drawn wagon was hammering down the road. Father ran out to see what was happening.

1 NARRATOR: The farmer climbed up on the hayrack to get a better view. Aldutė hid behind a haystack and watched.

ALDUTĖ: Men, women, and children sat in that wagon, blindfolded, and with their heads bowed. At the front and back of the wagon sat the White Armbanders with guns. More armed men rode alongside the wagon on bicycles. The wagon stopped just beyond a bend in the road. The families were ordered to climb out. At gun-point they were led to the crest of a hill where the fields meet dense forest. The families were ordered to undress. The farmer, his little girl, and the hired hand, soon could no longer see what was happening, but they could hear the screams and cries, which continued for a long time before the final gunshots came. The wagon came to a stop just beyond the bend in the road. The White Armbanders rammed their rifles into the people's backs and ordered them to climb up the hill. We heard screams and cries. That went on for a very long time. Who knows what went on there? Only much later, in the afternoon, we heard their final death cries and gunshots.

Gunshots. Darkness and silence.
The light slowly opens on stage grows. ALDUTĖ crawls out from under the table. She speaks softly.

ALDUTĖ: In the evening the men came to our farm house. They demanded vodka, although they were already very drunk. Our neighbor, Kazys Vaitkevičius, gave them everything he had. In exchange for the vodka they offered us shredded pillows. Later, everyone in the village was talking that they were searching for gold hidden in those pillows. Pillows were tossed everywhere along the roadside fences, and feathers from the pillows were scattered by the wind.

Music plays. The White Armbanders enter dancing a waltz together.

ALDUTĖ: For a long time those men hung around and sang. One blood-thirsty scoundrel began screaming hysterically and ran all the way back to Panemunėlis. He never returned to his right mind again after that. When they finally left to head back into the village, they beat their horses so badly with their whips that it was terrible to watch.

The WHITE ARMBANDERS dance a morbid hysterical dance. Then they grow tired and stumble down into the chairs. They tear off the white armbands and toss them on the floor. They sit with their heads bowed. The music grows steadily quieter. Then there is a pause.

1 NARRATOR: That day no one dared approach the killing site. The next day Šarkauskas and Vaitkevičius walked across the field to take a look. They found nine bodies dumped in a shallow grave on the hillock. Šarkauskas pushed his rake handle into the earth. The bodies were covered with only a few centimeters of soil. He dug poured more dirt over the bodies, forming a burial mound, so wild animals could not get to them.

EPILOGUE

Music. The NARRATORS rise from their seats. They gather up the papers from the stage floor. They place them onto the easels, covering the photographs.

1 NARRATOR: Beyond Three Hills
The Sun went down.
It was dusk
When we set out.

3 NARRATOR: A Black Angel
Carried off the Sun.
Beyond Three Hills
The Sun has set.

5 NARRATOR: Farewell, farewell—
We will never return—
We've already gone,
Beyond the Three Hills.

4 NARRATOR: And we did not find there
Our beloved Sun.
We only found
The dark night—
Beyond Three Hills
The Sun has set.

2 NARRATOR: Oh, farewell, farewell.
We will never return.
And flowers will bloom
In the early morning—
In the early morning,
We will never return.

The actors pick up the things that have been scattered around the stage. Respectfully, they place them on the table, forming the shape of a grave. They place Matilda's shoes on top of the grave.

2 NARRATOR:	Later we heard that they took the families of Noah Olkin and Mausha Jaffe out of the stable earlier than the others. Nine people in total.
3 NARRATOR:	Everyone talked about how the White Armbanders killed them sooner than the rest because they wanted to divide up their wealth.
1 NARRATOR:	Ilya Olkin was spared, but only for a short while. He met his bullet in the forests of Valkinkai. He managed to hide his fiance, Liza, in a convent among the nuns. She survived.
2 NARRATOR:	The people in the town of Panemunėlis knew who the killers were. The young people even made up a satirical song about one of them. He is dead now. Two of the others escaped to the West with the Nazis.
4 NARRATOR:	The next day, all 300 of Panemunėlis's Jews were brought to the ghetto in Rokiškis.
5 NARRATOR:	On the days of August 15th and 16th, 1941, in the forest, not far from the village of Bajorai, 3,200 Jews were shot and killed. Half of the population of Rokiškis.
2 NARRATOR:	Today, in the town of Rokiškis, not one descendant of the Litvak Jews remains alive **(places Grunia's stone on the table).**

The music grows quiet. We hear MATILDA singing a lullaby. The NARRATORS listen to her voice as though they were hearing an angel from heaven singing. The OLKIN family steps out onto the stage. MATILDA gathers the lillies from the easels. The rest of the family picks up the stones and carries them to the covered photographs. They place the stones around the photographs. Then they pause and stand respectfully beside the easels. Then, they sit back down in the center of the stage on the chairs, like they had when the play began.

1 NARRATOR: Matilda was barely nineteen years old when she died. She was only taking her very first steps as a poet. Those steps were both firm and fragile.

5 NARRATOR: Nobody knows how he managed it, but Noah Olkin passed on Matilda's notebook of poems and her diary to Father Matelionis. He hid them inside the altar of the Panemunėlis Church. Years later they were found by the church organist, Alfredas Andrijauskas. He passed them on to Dr. Irena Veisaitė, a Holocaust survivor and Professor of Literature.

2 NARRATOR: She was the first to speak out about the silenced muse, the poet who died too young, Matilda Olkin.

4 NARRATOR: It is a great loss that we only have a few fragments left from Matilda's life. A life that was short and tragic. It is our hope that Matilda's poems will travel out into the world and many others will one day read her words.

The NARRATOR steps out into the audience and hands out sheets of paper with Matilda's poems printed on them.

MATILDA: I hear the flowers quietly singing hymns.
And the angel's prayer rings out.
Oh Lord, in this wide world
I alone am voiceless.
And you will never know
My words and my prayers.
Only the white, white morning blossoms,
Will repeat my words at dawn to the Sun.

1 NARRATOR: They say that a poet is a prophet. And that a real poem is written not only by the poet's hand, but by...

Music grows louder. The rest of the actors step off stage and walk around the audience handing out Matilda's poems.

PRONUNCIATION GUIDE

Aldona – Al-do-nah
Aldutė – Al-du-te
Andrijauskas – An-dry-ow-skas
Apuokaitė - Ap-ow-kay-teh
Bajorai – Bah-yo-ray
Elijudis – Eli-you-dis
Genovaitė – Gen-oh-vay-teh
Grunia - Grun-ee-ah
Ilya – Il-yah
Kazys - Kah-zees
Kupiškis – Ku-pish-kis
Liudas Giras – Lou-das Gir-as
Neniškis - Ne-nish-kis
Panemunėlis – Pah-ne-mun-eh-lis
Panevėžys - Pah-neh-veh-zhys
Petronytė - Peh-tron-ee-teh
Rokiškis – Ro-kish-kis
Salomėja Nėris – Sal-oh-may-yah Ne-ris
Stasė Valavičiūtė – Sta-seh Va-la-vi-chut-eh
Šarkauskas - Shar-cow-skas
Šetekšna – She-tek-shna
Vaitkevičius- Vayt-kev-ich-yus
Vaitkūnas - Vit-koo-nahs
Valkinkai- Val-ki-nin-kay
Vytautas – Vee-taw-tas

Matilda Olkin

June 6, 1922 – July 10, 1941

The Olkin Sisters, Matilda, Mika, and Grunia with Liucija (Lucy)
Neniškytė. Panemunėlis, Lithuania

Playbill from the Lithuanian play, The Silenced Muses. Twenty-one performances in Lithuania between November 2016 and May 2018.

Viktorija Krivickaitė as Matilda in the Lithuanian production in 2016. Photograph by Darius Baltakys.

The playwright Neringa Danienė and her daughter, Eva, and translator Laima Vincė, visiting with Liucija (Lucy) Neniškytė, 94. Vilnius, Lithuania, June, 2018

Lithuanian actors portray the Olkin family. Front row: Sofia Pikasi as Grunia, Kęstutis Deksnys as Noah Olkin. Rima Bielovienė as Asna Olkin. Back row: Viktorija Krivickaitė as Matilda, Jokūbas Lukošiūnas as Ilya, and Meda Volkutė as Mika.

Made in the USA
Lexington, KY
06 March 2019